MW01625788

YOU'RE NEXT: START TODAY APPROACH

Transforming People, Businesses & Communities into LEADERS!

YOU'RE NEXT: START TODAY APPROACH

A PRODUCTIVITY MANAGEMENT TOOL

DR. SHANETTA WEATHERSPOON

R&W Leadership Services, LLC.
Lakewood, California

Published by R&W Leadership Services, LLC.
20611 Sylvanwood Avenue
Lakewood, California 90715

To my children, Nailah C. Robinson and Ray E. Robinson II, thank you for bearing with me. I love you both.

ACKNOWLEDGEMENTS

"Doing the best at this moment puts you in the best place for the next moment." – Oprah Winfrey

The productivity management tool is the result of being. In being, I cannot and will not say that I do all that I do alone. I have a very supportive village that continues to affirm every ambition, small or large. I would like to acknowledge all of my family, friends, sorors, cheerleaders, supporters, editors, colleagues, and peers over the years, you know who you are; THANK YOU! I would like to give thanks to God who has provided for and protected my children and me. As I reflect, the most relevant bible scripture is, "We are hard pressed on every side, but not crushed; perplexed, but not in despair; persecuted, but not abandoned; struck down, but not destroyed."- 2 Corinthians 4:9 With that I say again, THANK YOU for allowing me to do my best! This tool is for each of you who believe that effectiveness and productivity are magic; it is not! If I could do it, you can too.

INTRODUCTION

YOU'RE NEXT:
START TODAY APPROACH
A PRODUCTIVITY MANAGEMENT TOOL

"That's why I call my thing the marathon because I'm not gon' lie and portray this ultimate poise; like I been had it figured out. Nah, I just didn't quit! That's the only distinguishing quality from me and probably whoever else goin' through this or went through this or is gonna go through this is that I ain't quit! I went through every emotion! I went through every emotion with tryna pursue what I'm doing!"
– Airmiess Joseph Asghedom (Nipsey Hu$$le) in the song title, Perfect Ten, released June 2019.

Over the last 20 years, I have taken my StrengthsFinder personality development tool by Tom Rath at least four times. The results have always been consistent, indicating that I am both a maximizer and an activator. A maximizer values strengths. According to Gallup, "maximizers see talents and strengths in others, usually before anyone else does." We enjoy helping people realize what they are good at and thrive in and around excellence. "Excellence, not average, is their measure and pursuit. They have a quality orientation that leads them to focus on areas of strength for themselves and others and to manage around weakness." An activator is a person who thrives in action. According to Gallup, the recurring question for an activator is, "when do we start? Others may worry that there are still some things we don't know, but this doesn't seem to slow activators down." People around me would agree that these characteristics are representative of who I am, my value orientation, and my way of being. However, I never took the time to conceptualize the method of my effectiveness. Overtime and after reflection, I have grown to appreciate these strengths because they are the vehicle for my personal, academic, and professional productivity.

In doing the work to build the Start Today Approach, I noted a few provisos to the method. First, I am all about ACTION. I saw a quote online that read, "you do not need one hundred self-help books, you need action [to start TODAY] and discipline." I wholeheartedly agree with this notion. After successfully completing two years of coursework in my doctoral program, it was time to vet dissertation committee members. I recall thinking that it was important to select a person whose mode of operation was action-orientated (activator) and who had a solid research background (maximizer). Otherwise, I would be bogged down in tasks related to exploring ideas, which as we know are endless in academia. I knew what I wanted to research so the need was to have someone with the expertise to support getting started. Excited about an opportunity to work with one of my favorite professors, I requested a meeting with the one person who I thought would be a great fit based on her field of expertise. I recall sitting in her office presenting my topic, outline, and timeline for my research proposal. Mid-pitch, she stops me and states, "Shanetta, you need to be more reflective and explorative. I know that you are excited but six months is an unrealistic time frame to complete research that involves mixed method design." Although I respect my professor, I decided at that moment that she was not a good fit for my project. I ended up with another professor who supported my timeline and in the first meeting gave me articles to add to my research so that I can get started. The point of the story is, assuming that you are of sound mind to make decisions, once you've made a commitment or decided on something, whether it be a dissertation topic and theoretical framework, a new business idea, or the type of rug for the living room, it is counterproductive to second guess yourself or allow others to pause your movement under the pretense of 'reflection.' Sometimes, 'self-help books' could include people and the internet/social media, for example. You do not need hundreds of them when you have action and discipline.

Second, you find out more about who you are in times of pressure or past failure than you do in times of success. Times when you feel like you just can't get ahead are the times to glean the lessons from ancestors and past leadership gurus, which is to hold onto your purpose and core values. According to Ken Blanchard, a renowned business consultant, purpose is your "reason for existing, your why." Additionally, as my grandmother would say, "do not forget who you are."

Last but definitely not least, be both flexible and realistic with your time and goals. Life happens, change is inevitable and we are human. Discipline is not a destination or an activity, it is you holding to your own rules (e.g. core values) and being obedient to your purpose even when sh*t is going down around you. Discipline in this context is not a punishment, it is actually a reward. It is the gift of continuous consequences that is the vehicle for reaching your goals and being productive (i.e. the gift that keeps on giving).

It is also important to acknowledge that we are living in a time when people are valuing self-care just as much as productivity. This shift is very unique given that American culture is heavily performance-oriented, according to Northouse. Performance orientation emphasizes the attainment of goals and excellence which probably explains why the rates of depression, anxiety, and burnout are much higher amongst people who live in regional clusters with such values. This is fascinating to me because of the hundreds of leadership books that I have read, self-care and relationship building are the top themes that promote success or productivity yet seem to get lost in our day-to-day practice. The Start Today Approach takes self-care into account because it allows you the flexibility to change your mind and reset your goals according to your circumstances and needs while reinforcing the accomplishments along the way. One of my close colleagues, Desiree Rew, MBA MSW LCSW, created a cognitive behavior therapy model called Self-Care*ish AF. After attending one of her highly recommended webinars, I realized the simplest yet profound aspect of self-care is that it is what gives you energy and replenishes your tank. It is individual and looks different from person to person. Similarly, this journal will be your personal productivity management tool that will not only keep you on track but also considers self-care and relationship building. Let's get started TODAY!

PERSONAL PASSION

"Life doesn't come with an instruction manual. There is no 'right' way to live your life. What works for one person, may not work for another. What someone considers love, somebody else may not. What a person has planned for their life, may not end up the way they want. But you need to keep your head up, give life your best shot." – Thuy Le

Have you taken a personality assessment like the StrengthsFinder? If so, what were your results, and were they reflective of your personality? If not, make a plan to take one.

____

____

____

____

____

____

____

____

Have you ever felt stuck or a passion project stalled because you were seeking validation from others or bogged down in unnecessary research? If so, how can you prevent this stagnation in the future?

____

____

____

____

____

____

____

____

PART ONE: EFFECTIVENESS

"Make time for planning; wars are won in the general's tent."
– Stephen R. Covey in the book title, Seven Habits of Highly Effective People, released 2004.

The objective of the *Start Today Approach* is to improve productivity in order to reach short and long-term goals while tracking progress along the way. Productivity is a measure of effectiveness and/or success (i.e. the conversion of input to desired output). For example, if your goal is to spend more time with loved ones, input could include the effort put into hanging with those who you love and output is the number of times you actually made engagement happen. If you spent 4 more hours or days with loved ones this month than you did last month, then you have achieved your goal. The Start Today Approach imbeds goal development, encouragement, and reflection to increase individual effectiveness.

What do we know about effectiveness?

Similar to millions of other readers, my life changed when I read Stephen Covey's The Seven Habits of Highly Effective People. At the time, I was in my graduate program, a wife, a mother of two young children, and a full-time youth case worker with a host of other extended family and community obligations. Plus, I wanted to have fun and a social life too. Even though I was considerately effective, I needed to incorporate my future aspiration, like being a published author and purchasing my first home in my planning but I felt like the day-to-day was far more pressing and important at the time. Covey's time management matrix was the first step to my figuring out how to balance day-to-day responsibilities and long-term goals that would lead to future and sustainable success/life outcomes. For that I am grateful. The matrix provided by Covey helped to visually organize my activities (i.e. theoretical framework). All that I needed was a method to put the theory into practice that would offer room for evolution (i.e. the conceptual framework).

Symbols	Covey's Framework	Framework Description	Action (synthesize)
○	Quadrant I	Items that are both urgent and important. Examples include deadlines, crises, and emergencies.	Handle
◇	Quadrant II	Tasks that are not urgent but important to goal attainment, connected to balance and/or your purpose. Examples include spending time with family, exploring new opportunities, or building valuable business relationships.	Plan
△	Quadrant III	Activities that are unimportant but urgent. Examples include impromptu phone calls or meet-ups that are unplanned/unscheduled.	Delegate/Avoid
✕	Quadrant IV	Undertakings that are both unimportant and not urgent. Examples include engaging in drama or things that are a waste of time like mindless television or internet surfing outside of your free time.	Eliminate/Decrease

Adopted from Covey (2004)

PART TWO: PURPOSE

"Without a purpose, life is motion without meaning, activity without direction and events without reason. Without a purpose life is trivial, petty, and pointless." – Rick Warren

The first step is to outline your purpose by drafting your purpose statement. Recall, your purpose is the 'Why' for any action. It should be the overarching theme that permeates through every goal and the activities of your life whether personal, academic, or professional. Ask yourself the following questions:

What is my purpose? Why do I need to be more productive? What legacy am I attempting to attain? Who am I?

____

____

____

____

____

____

____

____

____

____

____

____

____

As you answer the purpose questions, you should notice some themes. These themes are often referred to as your core values (Blanchard & Stoner). Take some time to identify your core values. For example, my core values are loyalty, love, and empowerment toward others and myself.

1. ____
2. ____
3. ____

IMPORTANT: Take a day or two to become intimate with your purpose and core values before moving forward to the next phase. Purpose is so important to productivity. Many people find themselves hyperproductive but for the wrong reasons. Beyoncé's Break My Soul lyrics are so relatable because many people find themselves engaging in activities that reject their core values and do not feed their purpose, which leads to burnout, hopelessness, and regret. The lyrics give people permission to take a step back to refocus on the things that are important.

PART THREE: GOAL SETTING

"The trouble with not having a goal is that you can spend your life running up and down the field and never score." – Bill Copeland

We have all heard of S.M.A.R.T. goals because the concept has been around since 1981 when introduced by George T. Doran in the article, "There's a S.M.A.R.T. Way to Write Management Goals and Objectives." The acronym stands for specific, manageable, attainable, relevant, and timely. The reason this method is so transferable from organizational to personal goal setting is that it supports organizing your thoughts and motivations to start today. Additionally, the S.M.A.R.T. method is a measurement tool because it will allow you to track your progress once you start. Practice building S.M.A.R.T. goals to manage your quadrant one and two tasks. An example of a S.MA.R.T. quadrant two goal is as follows:

- I will start a business training athletes by spending two hours a week on planning, research and development (Specific and Measurable). I have been playing basketball for over 20 years, coaching students for at least ten of those years and have built the reputation and relationships to support this business (Attainable). I am passionate about basketball and love mentoring at-risk youth (Relevant). I will file the paperwork to incorporate and enroll five students within three months from today (Timely).

Practice creating S.M.A.R.T. goals because they will be your guide to productivity.

____

____

____

____

____

____

____

____

____

____

____

For your quadrant two, the most important area and focal point for productivity, you should include BHAGs. BHAGs are Big Hairy Audacious Goals. Even though BHAGs are not related directly to money (i.e. the bag), it is the vehicle through which you can build both personal and organizational capital while connecting to your core purpose. This term was introduced by Jim Collins and Jerry Porras in their 1994 book, "*Built to Last: Successful Habits of Visionary Companies.*" A BHAG is your opportunity to be creative and work toward a goal that even you would think is unimaginable. It incorporates an 'ah' factor and is in some ways both attainable and unattainable. Some popular examples of BHAGs include:

- Starbucks: Become the most recognized & respected consumer brand in the world.
- Disneyland: Be the happiest place on earth.
- Amazon: Every book, ever printed, in any language, all available in less than 60 seconds.

Your BHAGs should excite you, relate to your core values and purpose, and be very specific.

What are your BHAGs?

____

____

____

____

____

____

____

____

____

____

____

____

____

____

____

____

PART FOUR: START TODAY APPROACH

"Achievement requires commitment."
– Dr. Shanetta Weatherspoon

Instructions. The You're Next: Start Today Approach is a productivity management tool that assists users in organizing their to-do lists across time frames and priorities. The goal of the Start Today Approach is to grant you the flexibility and autonomy to move your obligations around given the uncertainty of life without surging up anxiety and feelings of uselessness. It is simple, we are using the thought process of the most credible scholars and practitioners to create a daily to-do list. Take what we have learned from Covey, Collins, Doran, Blanchard, etc. to organize your day. Write out your to-do list, and try to include all tasks across the quadrants. Use the key above to conceptualize the priority area of the task. Remember that quadrant two tasks are essential to productivity according to Covey, so include those on the list. If you do not finish your to-do list today, simply start again tomorrow by including those tasks on that list and adding more if you feel energized. After 12 days, tally your productivity. Remember you are the judge of your progress, this approach is just to help track your productivity (i.e. effectiveness/success).

Goal **Task Notes** Date: 04/07/2022

○ ~~*Draft an email about the NAACP to send to GCLA.*~~
△ *Take Ares (dog) to the vet.*
✕ ~~*Answer unplanned calls for two hours per day (DND).*~~
○ ~~*Pay tuition.*~~
○ *Register for the conference before April 10th deadline.*
◇ *Start the manuscript for the biography/create Wiki page.*
✕ ~~*Social media binges.*~~
◇ ~~*Lunch with CEO of TASKS (potential non profit partner).*~~

12 Day Check-In

Symbols	Covey's Quadrant	Completed	Remaining
○	I (Handle)	2	1
◇	II (Plan)	1	1
△	III (Delegate/Avoid)	0	1
✕	IV (Eliminate/Decrease)	2	0

Goal **Task Notes** Date: __/__/____

Goal **Task Notes** Date: __/__/____

Goal **Task Notes** Date: __/__/____

Goal **Task Notes** Date: __/__/____

Goal **Task Notes** Date: __/__/____

Goal **Task Notes** Date: __/__/____

Goal **Task Notes** Date: __/__/____

Goal **Task Notes** Date: __/__/____

Goal **Task Notes** Date: __/__/____

Goal **Task Notes** Date: __/__/____

Goal **Task Notes** Date: __/__/____

Goal **Task Notes** Date: __/__/____

12 Day Check-In

Symbols	Covey's Quadrant	Completed	Remaining
○	I (Handle)		
◇	II (Plan)		
△	III (Delegate/Avoid)		
✕	IV (Eliminate/Decrease)		

“It is always the right time to start.” – Charlotte White

Goal **Task Notes** Date: __/__/____

Goal **Task Notes** Date: __/__/____

Goal **Task Notes** Date: __/__/____

Goal **Task Notes** Date: __/__/____

Goal **Task Notes** Date: __/__/____

Goal **Task Notes** Date: __/__/____

Goal **Task Notes** Date: __/__/____

Goal **Task Notes** Date: __/__/____

Goal **Task Notes** Date: __/__/____

Goal **Task Notes** Date: __/__/____

Goal **Task Notes** Date: __/__/____

Goal **Task Notes** Date: __/__/____

12 Day Check-In

Symbols	Covey's Quadrant	Completed	Remaining
○	I (Handle)		
◇	II (Plan)		
△	III (Delegate/Avoid)		
✗	IV (Eliminate/Decrease)		

"Life is like riding a bicycle, to keep your balance you must keep moving." – Albert Einstein

Goal **Task Notes** Date: __/__/____

Goal **Task Notes** Date: __/__/____

Goal **Task Notes** Date: __/__/____

Goal **Task Notes** Date: __/__/____

Goal **Task Notes** Date: __/__/____

Goal **Task Notes** Date: __/__/____

Goal **Task Notes** Date: __/__/____

Goal **Task Notes** Date: __/__/____

Goal **Task Notes** Date: __/__/____

Goal **Task Notes** Date: __/__/____

Goal **Task Notes** Date: __/__/____

Goal **Task Notes** Date: __/__/____

12 Day Check-In

Symbols	Covey's Quadrant	Completed	Remaining
○	I (Handle)		
◇	II (Plan)		
△	III (Delegate/Avoid)		
✗	IV (Eliminate/Decrease)		

"Comparison is the best way to judge our progress ...but not with others, compare your yesterday with your today..." – Agboola Kehinde Solomon

Goal **Task Notes** Date: __/__/____

Goal **Task Notes** Date: __/__/____

Goal **Task Notes** Date: __/__/____

Goal **Task Notes** Date: __/__/____

Goal **Task Notes** Date: __/__/____

Goal **Task Notes** Date: __/__/____

Goal **Task Notes** Date: __/__/____

Goal **Task Notes** Date: __/__/____

Goal **Task Notes** Date: __/__/____

Goal	Task Notes	Date: __/__/____

Goal **Task Notes** Date: __/__/____

Goal **Task Notes** Date: __/__/____

_____ ____
____
____
_____ ____
____
____
_____ ____
____
____
_____ ____
____
____
_____ ____
____
____
_____ ____
____
____
_____ ____
____
____
_____ ____
____
____
_____ ____
____
____

12 Day Check-In

Symbols	Covey's Quadrant	Completed	Remaining
○	I (Handle)		
◇	II (Plan)		
△	III (Delegate/Avoid)		
✗	IV (Eliminate/Decrease)		

"Without commitment, you'll never start. But more importantly, without consistency, you'll never finish." – Denzel Washington

Goal **Task Notes** Date: __/__/____

____ ____

____

____

____ ____

____

____

____ ____

____

____

____ ____

____

____

____ ____

____

____

____ ____

____

____

____ ____

____

____

____ ____

____

____

____ ____

____

____

____ ____

____

____

Goal **Task Notes** Date: __/__/____

Goal **Task Notes** Date: __/__/____

Goal **Task Notes** Date: __/__/____

Goal **Task Notes** Date: __/__/____

Goal **Task Notes** Date: __/__/____

Goal **Task Notes** Date: __/__/____

Goal **Task Notes** Date: __/__/____

Goal **Task Notes** Date: __/__/____

Goal **Task Notes** Date: __/__/____

Goal **Task Notes** Date: __/__/____

Goal **Task Notes** Date: __/__/____

12 Day Check-In

Symbols	Covey's Quadrant	Completed	Remaining
○	I (Handle)		
◇	II (Plan)		
△	III (Delegate/Avoid)		
✗	IV (Eliminate/Decrease)		

PART FIVE: RECOMMENDATIONS

"A book is a gift you can open again and again." – Garrison

Collectively, I have over 12 years of post-secondary education, not including conferences, training, and certifications. Additionally, I have been teaching courses with a foundation in leadership, personal identity development, and motivation since 2013. In each of the courses, I offer a list of books for students to read if they so choose. These recommendations are made up of books that I have read and/or colleagues in the field recommend. I have read over two-thirds of the selections and believe that they have been helpful to continued productivity. I would not recommend them if I did not think that they would be beneficial to your productivity. In academia, this list would be considered a reference page for the *Start Today Approach*. The hope is that this recommended reading list motivates you to continue to expand your mind, craft your goals, and evolve. The book titles with an asterisk mark were the most useful on my journey.

I challenge you to complete this list. Check off the ones you read as you go.

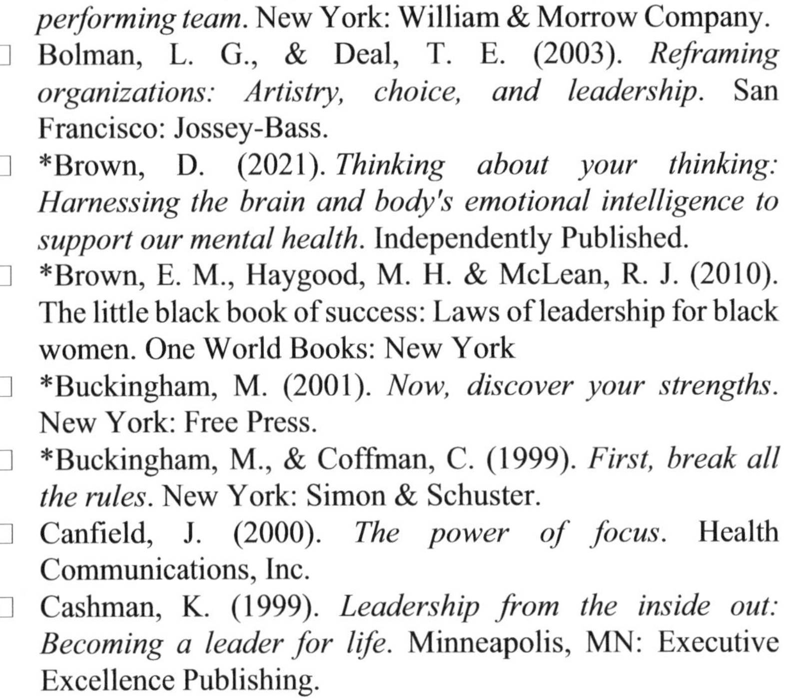

- ☐ Blanchard, K. (2000). *The one minute manager builds high performing team*. New York: William & Morrow Company.
- ☐ Bolman, L. G., & Deal, T. E. (2003). *Reframing organizations: Artistry, choice, and leadership*. San Francisco: Jossey-Bass.
- ☐ *Brown, D. (2021). *Thinking about your thinking: Harnessing the brain and body's emotional intelligence to support our mental health*. Independently Published.
- ☐ *Brown, E. M., Haygood, M. H. & McLean, R. J. (2010). The little black book of success: Laws of leadership for black women. One World Books: New York
- ☐ *Buckingham, M. (2001). *Now, discover your strengths*. New York: Free Press.
- ☐ *Buckingham, M., & Coffman, C. (1999). *First, break all the rules*. New York: Simon & Schuster.
- ☐ Canfield, J. (2000). *The power of focus*. Health Communications, Inc.
- ☐ Cashman, K. (1999). *Leadership from the inside out: Becoming a leader for life*. Minneapolis, MN: Executive Excellence Publishing.

- Coles, R. (2001). *Lives of moral leadership*. New York: Random House.
- *Collins, J. (2001). *Good to great: Why some companies make the leap... and others don't*. New York: Harper Collins.
- *Covey, S. (2004). *The 8th Habit: From effectiveness to greatness*. New York: Free Press.
- *Covey, S. (1989). *The seven habits of highly effective people.* New York: Simon & Schuster.
- DePree, M. (1993). *Leadership jazz*. New York: Bantam Dell.
- DePree, M. (1990). *Leadership is an art*. New York: Bantam Dell.
- *Elliott, C. (2022). *I love me, intentionally!: 10 transformational principles to loving you first.* Catrena Elliott.
- Frankl, V. (2000). *Man's search for meaning*. Boston, MA: Beacon Press.
- *Gladwell, M. (2000). *The tipping point! How little things can make a big difference*. New York: Little Brown & Company.
- Goldsmith, M. (2000). *Coaching for leadership.* San Francisco: Jossey Bass.
- Goleman, D. (2002). *Primal leadership.* Boston, MA: Harvard Business School Publishing.
- *Goleman, D. (2000). *Working with Emotional Intelligence*. New York: Bantam Books.
- Heifetz, R. A., & Linsky, M. (2002). *Leadership on the line*. Boston, MA: Harvard Business School Publishing.
- *Helgesen, S. (1995). *The female advantage: Women's way of leadership*. New York: Currency.
- Hill, M.S., & Ragland, J. C. (1995). *Women as educational leaders*. Thousand Oaks, CA: Corwin Press.
- *Johnson, S. (1998). *Who moved my cheese?* New York: Putnam Publishing Group.
- Jones, L. B. (1995). *Jesus: CEO*. New York: Random House.
- Katzenback, J. (2000). *Peak performance*. Boston, MA: Harvard Business School Publishing.
- Kotter, J. P. (1999). *On what leaders really do*. Boston, MA: Harvard Business School Publishing.
- Kouzes, J. M., & Posner, B. Z. (2002). *The leadership challenge*. San Francisco: Jossey Bass.
- Maister, D. (2000). *True professionalism.* New York: Touchstone Books.

- Maslow, A. (1998). *Maslow on management.* New York: John Wiley & Sons.
- McCormick, B., & Davenport, D. (2003). *Shepherd leadership: Wisdom for leaders from Psalms 23 shepherd leadership*. San Francisco: Jossey-Bass.
- O'Neil, J. (1994). *The paradox of success*. New York: Penguin-Putnam, Inc.
- O'Toole, J. (1995). *Leading change – value based leadership*. New York: Ballantine Books.
- Palmer, P. (2004). *A hidden wholeness: The journey toward an undivided life*. San Francisco: Jossey-Bass.
- Rand, A. (1996). *Atlas shrugged.* New York: Penguin-Putnam, Inc.
- *Rath, Tom; (2007). Strenghts Finder 2.0; Ney York, NY. Gallup Press.
- *Robinson, K. (2001). *Out of our minds: Learning to be creative*. West Sussex: Capstone Publishing Limited.
- Sample, S. B. (2002). *The contrarian's guide to leadership*. San Francisco: Jossey-Bass.
- Seifter, H., & Economy, P. (2001). *Leadership ensemble: Lessons in collaborative management from the world's only conductorless orchestra*. New York: Times Books.
- Senge, P. (1990). *The fifth discipline: The art and practice of learning organizations*. New York: Doubleday.
- Senn, L. (1999). *The secrets of a winning culture*. Canada: The Leadership Press.
- Thrall, B. (1999). *The ascent of a leader*. San Francisco: Jossey-Bass.
- Tutu, D. (2004). *God has a dream: A vision of hope for our time*. New York: Doubleday.
- Ulrich, D., Zenger, J., & Smallwood, N. (1999). *Results-based leadership*. Boston, MA: Harvard Business School Publishing.
- Watson, A. W., & Brown, K. (2001). *The most effective organizations in the U.S.* New York: Random House.
- *Zander, R., & Zander, B. (2000). *The art of possibility*. New York: Penguin Books.

~~THE END~~

KEEP GOING!

Made in the USA
Monee, IL
10 May 2023

3c3520ba-9e2e-4f72-8e88-1d6a56ec135dR01